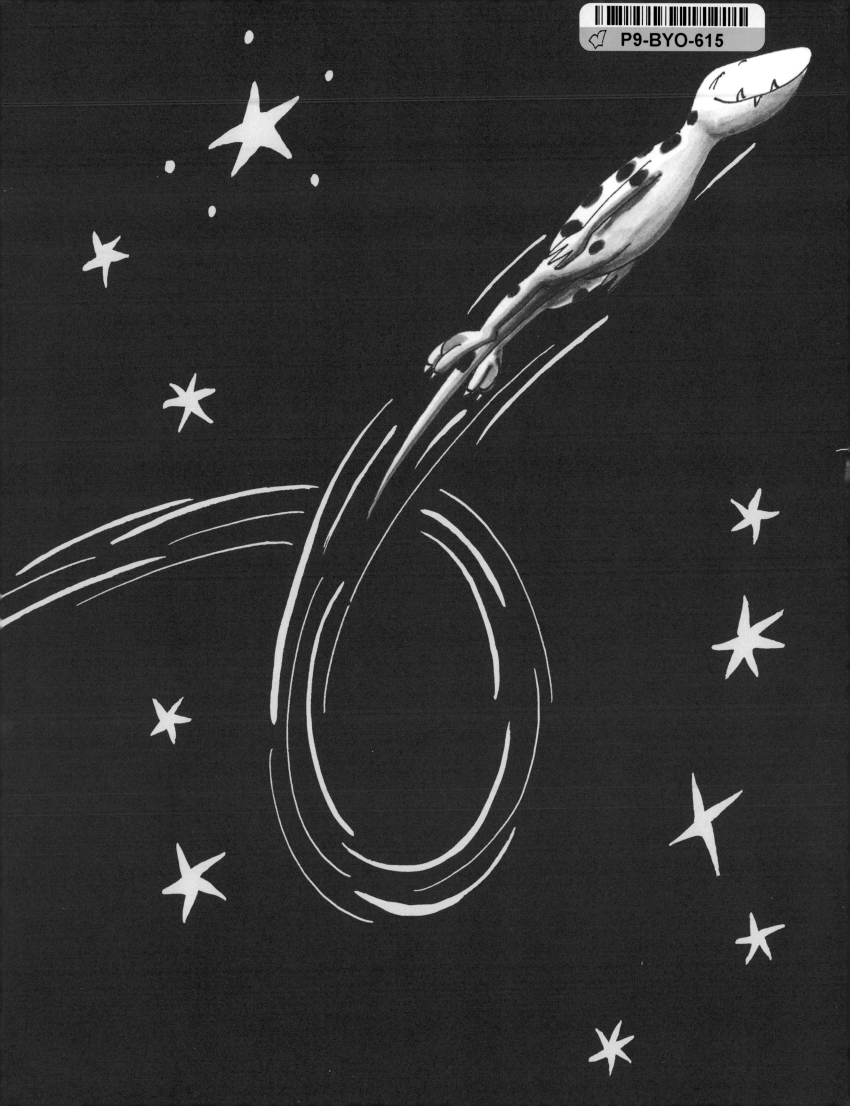

Dinosaurumpus!

For Maud, Milly, and Ben
— T. M.

For Sarah, with love
— G. P-R.

Text copyright © 2002 by Tony Mitton
Illustrations copyright © 2002 by Guy Parker-Rees

First published in Great Britain in 2002 by Orchard Books London

Library of Congress Cataloging-in-Publication Data available.
ISBN-13: 978-0-439-39514-4 / ISBN-10: 0-439-39514-3

10 9 8 7 6   09 10 11 12 13
Printed in China
First edition, March 2003

Dinosaurumpus!

By Tony Mitton

Illustrated by Guy Parker-Rees

ORCHARD BOOKS ∞ NEW YORK
AN IMPRINT OF SCHOLASTIC INC.

There's a quake and a quiver
and a rumbling around.

It makes you shiver.
It's a thundery sound.

"Shake, shake, shudder...
near the sludgy old swamp.
The dinosaurs are coming.
Get ready to romp.

Donk!

Donk!

Donk!

Here's **Triceratops** jumping UP and DOWN doing dinosaur hops.

He wears three horns
on his **big**, bony head,

and thunders along with a
Bomp! Bomp! tread.

"Shake, shake, shudder...
near the sludgy old swamp.
The dinosaurs are coming.
Get ready to romp..."

Watch out for
Deinosuchus
with her
snip-snap grin,
as she perches
on her tail and
twists
in a spin.

Apatosaurus stops
for a slushy, mushy snack.
His tail starts swinging with a

Thwack! Thwack! Thwack!

"Shake, shake, shudder"...
near the sludgy old swamp.
The dinosaurs are coming.
Get ready to romp.

Pteranodon dives with a swift, sharp swoop. He shrieks out an Eeeeeek! as he swirls in a loop.

Stegosaurus stomps along
with lots of her playmates.

Clatter! Clatter! Clatter!

go their bony
back plates.

"Shake, shake, shudder"...
near the sludgy old swamp.
The dinosaurs are coming.
Get ready to romp.

Styracosaurus shakes
his collar and his spikes.
Rattle! Rattle! Rattle!
is the noise that he likes!

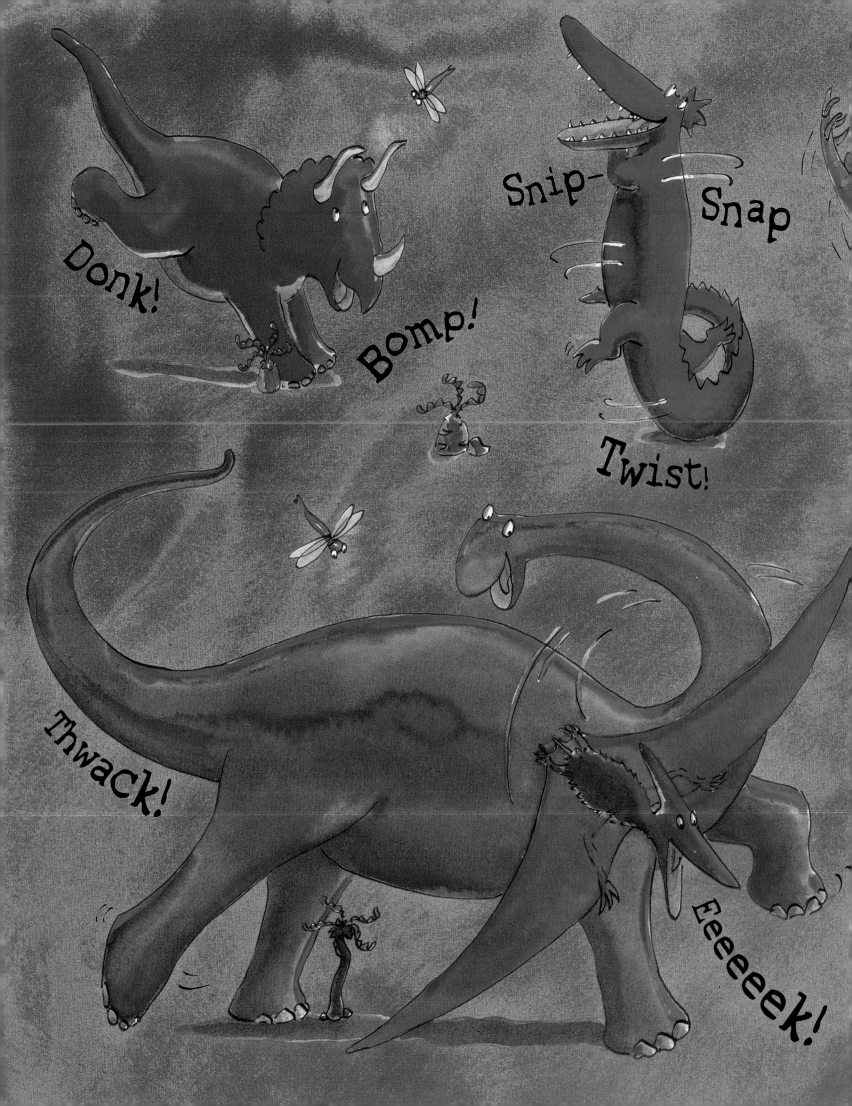

Clatter!

Rattle!

Zoom! Zoom!

Come and take a peek....

"Shake, shake, shudder...
near the sludgy old swamp.
Everybody's doing the
dinosaur romp.

rrrrr...!

Roar! Roar! Roar!
Now we're shivering with fright.
What can make a noise like that
in the night?

He's huge
and he's **heavy**,
but all he wants to do...

"Shake, shake, shudder"...
near the sludgy old swamp.
Everybody's doing the
dinosaur romp.

The dinosaurs won't scratch us,
or bite us, or thump us.
They just want to holler up a...

rumpus!

"Shake, shake, shudder...
near the sludgy old swamp.
Everybody's doing the
dinosaur romp.

A dinosaurumpus
gives a **Sizzle!**
and a
zing!

But soon all the rompers grow sleepy and slow.

The rumpus calms down and the sound drops low.

The rompers drift together
and tumble in a heap...

'til finally the dinosaurs
are all fast asleep.

And now the only noise
in the deep of the night
is...

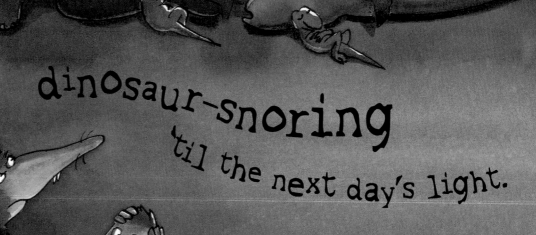

dinosaur-snoring
'til the next day's light.